LOS ANGELES LAKERS

ALL-TIME GREATS

BY BRENDAN FLYNN

Book design by Jake Slavik
Cover design by Jake Slavik

Photographs ©: Nuccio DiNuzzo/AP Images, cover (top), 1 (top); Mark Terrill/AP Images, cover (bottom), 1 (bottom); Bettmann/Getty Images, 4, 9; Minnesota Historical Society/ Corbis Historical/Getty Images, 6; Focus on Sport/Getty Images, 10, 12; Peter Read Miller/ Sports Illustrated/SetNumber: X30112 TK3 R10 F11/Getty Images, 15; Manny Millan/Sports Illustrated/Set Number: X31552/Getty Images, 16; Wally Skalij/Los Angeles Times/Getty Images, 18; Jim McIsaac/Getty Images Sport/Getty Images, 20; Red Line Editorial, 22

Press Box Books, an imprint of Press Room Editions.

ISBN
978-1-63494-156-3 (library bound)
978-1-63494-169-3 (paperback)
978-1-63494-182-2 (epub)
978-1-63494-195-2 (hosted ebook)

Library of Congress Control Number: 2019951058

Distributed by North Star Editions, Inc.
2297 Waters Drive
Mendota Heights, MN 55120
www.northstareditions.com

Printed in the United States of America
012020

ABOUT THE AUTHOR

Brendan Flynn is a San Francisco resident and an author of numerous children's books. In addition to writing about sports, Flynn also enjoys competing in triathlons, Scrabble tournaments, and chili cook-offs.

TABLE OF CONTENTS

MIKAN
99
LAKERS
99

CHAPTER 1

PIONEERS

The Los Angeles Lakers were one of the NBA's original teams. Except they didn't play in Los Angeles. They were in Minneapolis. The Lakers were the first NBA dynasty. They won four of the first five league championships in the early 1950s. And they had the league's first star player.

Center **George Mikan** was the main attraction for the Lakers. The 6'10" center towered over his opponents. All around the league, fans filled arenas to watch him dominate. Mikan had an excellent hook

MIKKELSEN
19
POLLARD
17

shot with either hand. He led the NBA in scoring twice. He also led the league in rebounding twice.

Mikan’s teammates on the front line were power forward **Vern Mikkelsen** and small forward **Jim Pollard**. Mikkelsen was an intense defender and rebounder. At 6'7" tall, Mikkelsen was tough to stop inside. And he was durable too. He only missed five games over his 10-year career.

Pollard was an outstanding athlete. His amazing jumping ability led to his nickname, “the Kangaroo Kid.” He also was an excellent shooter, especially from the corner. He and Mikkelsen teamed with Mikan on all four Lakers championship teams.

In 1958–59, forward **Elgin Baylor** made quite a splash for the Lakers. He won the NBA Rookie of the Year Award after he averaged 24.9 points per game. Baylor could shoot from any angle. He could score from anywhere on the court. He was an outstanding dribbler and passer too.

Baylor spent two seasons in Minneapolis with the Lakers. He led the team in scoring and made the All-Star team in both seasons. Then the team moved to Los Angeles and Baylor's career took off. In 1961–62 he set career highs with 38.3 points and 13.1 rebounds per game.

STAT SPOTLIGHT

MOST CAREER REBOUNDS

LAKERS TEAM RECORD

Elgin Baylor: 11,463

BAYLOR
22

WEST
44

MIKAN DRILL

George Mikan popularized a practice routine that big players still use today. In the Mikan Drill, a player stands under the hoop and shoots a right-handed layup. Then the player grabs the rebound and does the same on the other side of the basket. It helps players develop their skills with both hands.

In their first season out west, the Lakers drafted point guard **Jerry West**. West and Baylor were one of the NBA's top scoring duos of the 1960s. West had a deadly jump shot and was fueled by a competitive fire that few could match. He averaged more than 25 points per game in 11 straight seasons.

The Lakers reached the NBA Finals seven times between 1962 and 1970. But they kept falling short. Finally, in 1971–72, West and center **Wilt Chamberlain** teamed up to lead the Lakers to a championship.

JOHNSON
32

CHAPTER 2
SHOWTIME

After finally breaking through in the 1970s, the Lakers dominated the '80s. They won five NBA titles between 1980 and 1988. And they did it in style. The Lakers were known for a fast-paced offense that showed off the skills of their many talented players. The team even picked up a nickname along the way. They were called "Showtime," because Lakers games were the place to be in Los Angeles.

Magic Johnson was Showtime's ringleader. When he was a rookie, the Lakers reached the 1980 NBA Finals. In Game 6,

STAT SPOTLIGHT

SINGLE-SEASON ASSISTS PER GAME

LAKERS TEAM RECORD

Magic Johnson: 13.1 (1983-84)

Johnson scored a season-high 42 points and grabbed 15 rebounds to beat the Philadelphia 76ers and clinch the title.

That was a sign of things to come for Johnson. He redefined the point guard position in the NBA. Standing 6'9" tall, he could guard forwards and centers. But his passing and dribbling skills were the envy of other guards. Johnson won the NBA Most Valuable Player (MVP) Award three times.

SHOWTIME CO-STARS

Sweet-shooting forward **James Worthy** and unsung grinder **A. C. Green** played supporting roles on the front lines in the 1980s. Meanwhile in the backcourt, **Byron Scott** rained down three-pointers and **Michael Cooper** played shutdown defense.

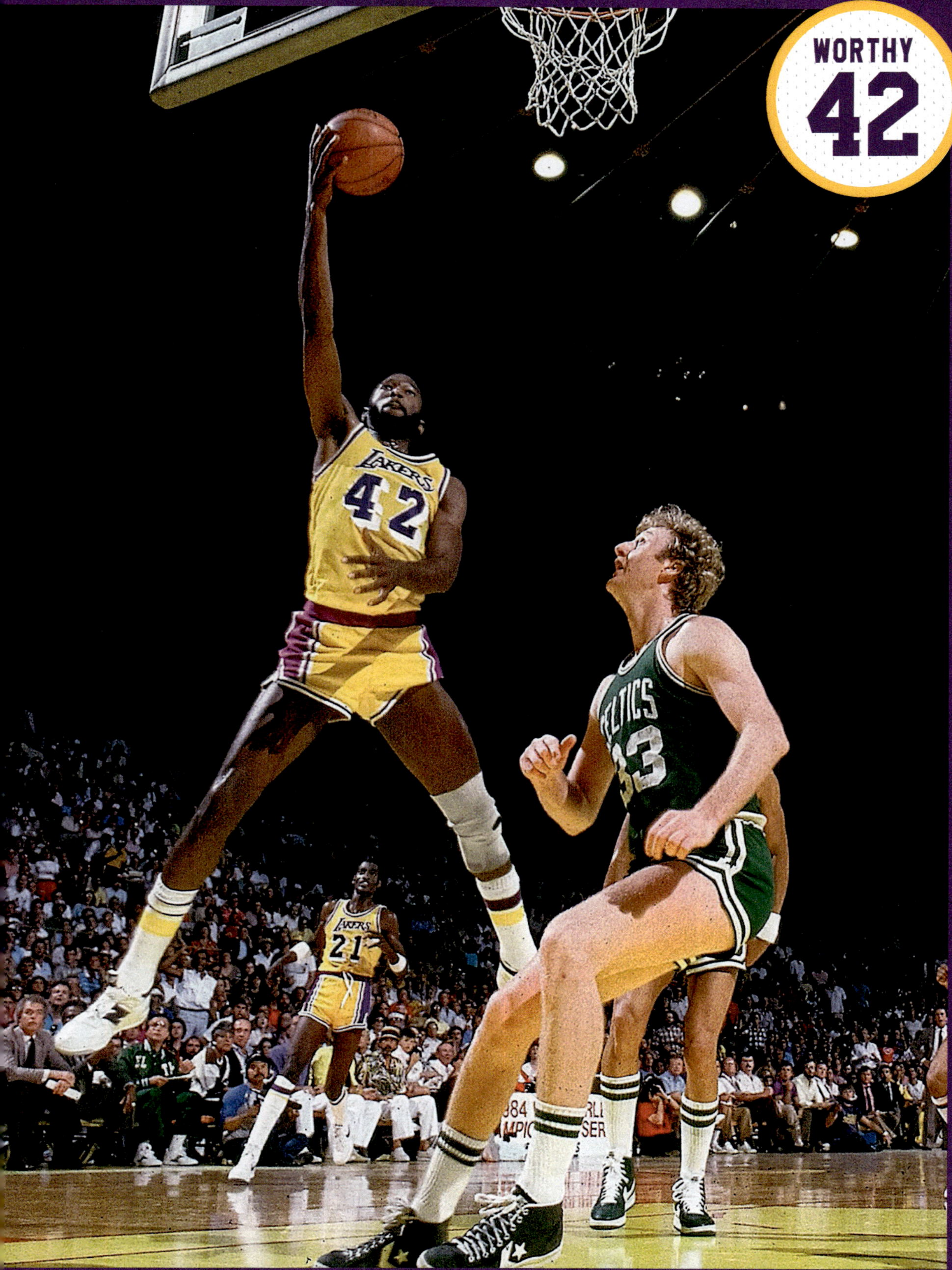
WORTHY
42
LAKERS
42
LAKERS
21

ABDUL-JABBAR
33

The 12-time All-Star was named the NBA Finals MVP three times too.

Johnson led the NBA in assists four times. Many of those passes went to **Kareem Abdul-Jabbar**. The lanky center holds many NBA career records, including most points and minutes played.

Abdul-Jabbar's go-to shot was his "sky hook." It was a hook shot that was impossible to block, partly because he was 7'2" tall. He also wore goggles after being poked in the eye multiple times. They worked well. Abdul-Jabbar was a six-time NBA MVP and played until he was 42 years old.

STAT SPOTLIGHT

MOST CAREER POINTS

NBA LEAGUE RECORD

Kareem Abdul-Jabbar: 38,387

O'NEAL
34
BRYANT
8
LAKERS
8

CHAPTER 3

MODERN STARS

The Lakers soon built another dynasty that won five NBA titles in 11 seasons. In 1999–2000 they won the first of three straight championships. That team was led by two future Hall of Famers.

Center **Shaquille O'Neal** and guard **Kobe Bryant** were that era's stars. At 7'1" and 325 pounds, O'Neal was hard to miss. He was known for his outsized personality and thunderous dunks. His size made him almost unstoppable in the post. O'Neal led the NBA in field goal percentage 10 times in his

19-year career. O'Neal left Los Angeles in 2004 and won another title in Miami.

Bryant played 20 seasons in the NBA, all with the Lakers. He was a volume scorer who also played strong defense. Bryant once scored 81 points in a game, and he won two league scoring titles. Bryant led the Lakers to NBA championships in 2008–09 and 2009–10.

After winning NBA titles in Miami and Cleveland, **LeBron James** joined the Lakers in 2018. He's considered by many to be the greatest player of his generation. James is a bruising power forward with the skills of a guard. Then dynamic center **Anthony Davis** arrived by trade before the 2019–20 season. The Lakers appeared to have the pieces in place to challenge for another title in Los Angeles.

STAT SPOTLIGHT

MOST CAREER GAMES

LAKERS TEAM RECORD

Kobe Bryant: 1,346

TIMELINE

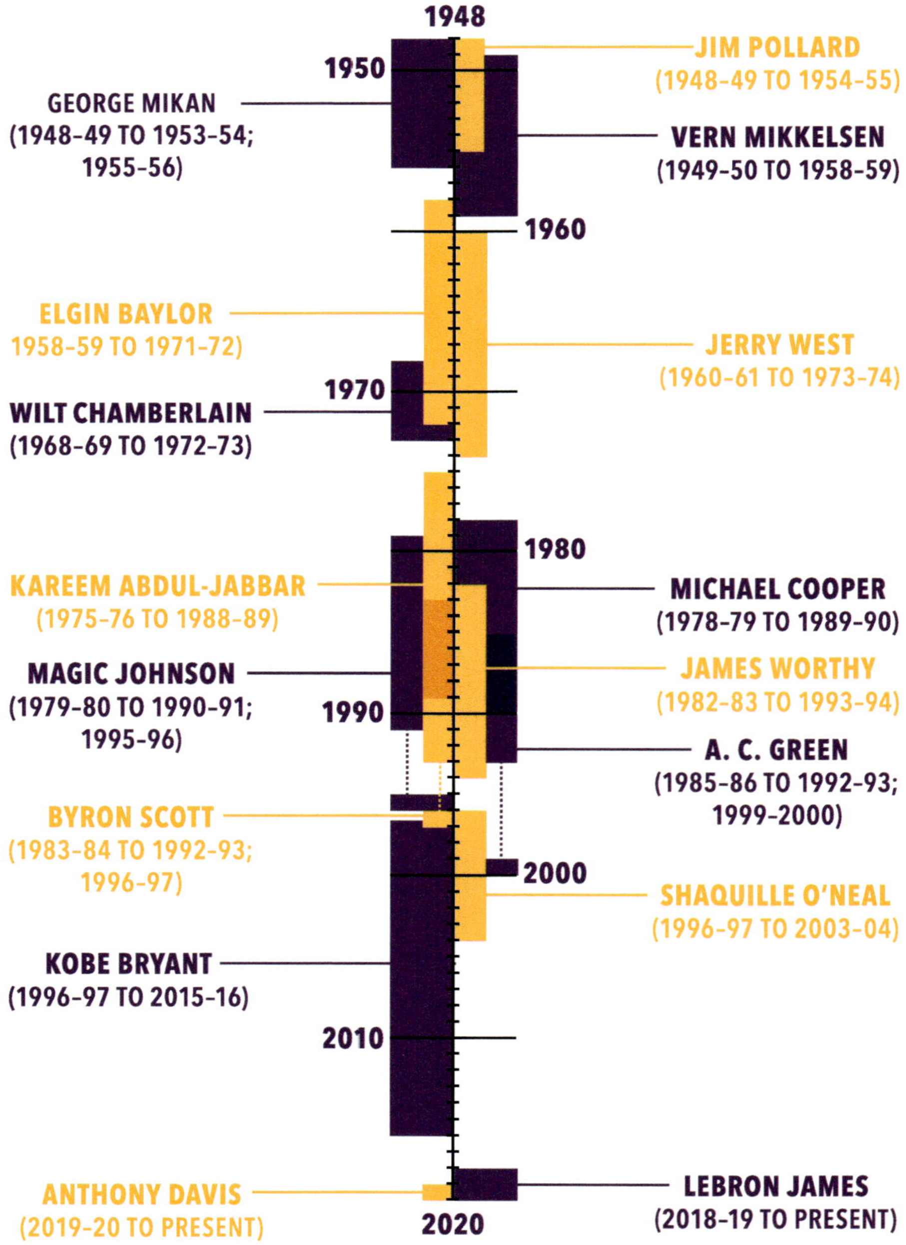
1948
1950
1960
1970
1980
1990
2000
2010
2020
JIM POLLARD
(1948-49 TO 1954-55)
GEORGE MIKAN
(1948-49 TO 1953-54;
1955-56)
VERN MIKKELSEN
(1949-50 TO 1958-59)
ELGIN BAYLOR
1958-59 TO 1971-72)
JERRY WEST
(1960-61 TO 1973-74)
WILT CHAMBERLAIN
(1968-69 TO 1972-73)
KAREEM ABDUL-JABBAR
(1975-76 TO 1988-89)
MICHAEL COOPER
(1978-79 TO 1989-90)
MAGIC JOHNSON
(1979-80 TO 1990-91;
1995-96)
JAMES WORTHY
(1982-83 TO 1993-94)
A. C. GREEN
(1985-86 TO 1992-93;
1999-2000)
BYRON SCOTT
(1983-84 TO 1992-93;
1996-97)
SHAQUILLE O'NEAL
(1996-97 TO 2003-04)
KOBE BRYANT
(1996-97 TO 2015-16)
ANTHONY DAVIS
(2019-20 TO PRESENT)
LEBRON JAMES
(2018-19 TO PRESENT)

TEAM FACTS

LOS ANGELES LAKERS

Formerly: Minneapolis Lakers (1949 to 1960)

First NBA season: 1949–50

NBA championships: 15

Key coaches:

Phil Jackson (1999–2000 to 2010–11)
610–292, 118–63 playoffs, 5 NBA titles

John Kundla (1949–50 to 1958–59)
423–302, 60–35 playoffs, 5 NBA titles

Pat Riley (1981–82 to 1989–90) 533–194,
102–47 playoffs, 4 NBA titles

MORE INFORMATION

To learn more about the Los Angeles Lakers, go to **pressboxbooks.com/AllAccess**.

These links are routinely monitored and updated to provide the most current information available.

Through 2018–19 season

GLOSSARY

assist
A pass that leads directly to a basket.

durable
Tough, long-lasting.

dynamic
Energetic, creating positive change.

dynasty
A team that has an extended period of success, usually winning multiple championships in the process.

hook shot
A one-handed shot in which a player extends one arm out to the side and over the head toward the basket.

intense
Extremely earnest or serious.

point guard
The player who directs a team's offensive attack.

rookie
A first-year player.

unsung
Rarely praised or given credit.

INDEX